Pick Your Own

Amanda Bonnick

thank you for your support!

Lots of love

Amanda Bonnick x

Pick Your Own

Amanda Bonnick
Edited by Black Pear Press

First published in March 2019 by Black Pear Press
www.blackpear.net

ISBN 978-1-910322-93-2

Cover Photograph and Design by Amanda Bonnick and Black Pear Press

Acknowledgements

My sincere thanks to all my beta-readers, reviewers and friends for the amazing support and invaluable advice as I've put this pamphlet together. There are too many of you to mention individually. You know who you are.

Amanda

Dedication

To my father

My Father

The earthgrip holds him
tight, unyielding, best fit ever.
The wordhoard told of him
bright, golden, kindly, clever.
My heartsache misses him
loving, tender, young forever.

Contents

First

First I have to describe the door
that I slammed behind me,
pale purple, number fifty-three,
set in a 30s bungalow,
front lawn, too small to play on.

Tall thin gate on the exciting side,
slipway between this house and the next,
almost magic, almost somewhere else,
where cats hide their kills
and burglars trip on old bikes.
The boring side, a parked sports car,
could be red, green or orange,
I've lost count; each too small
to carry children comfortably.
A 'wish life had been different' car.

But no, first let me describe
the drive that leads to the gate.
It is gravel; shades of stone
crunch under each step,
drained of colour by the sun.
Timid flowers appear here and there,
bullied by weeds.

Then I must describe the house.
How many bedrooms are there?
Four, of course.
One for the mother and her fancy men,
one for the boy with all his toys.
We three girls arrange ourselves
in the ill-fitting remainder.

contd…

contd…

But no, first I must describe the mother
who keeps us in this house.
Beautiful, desperate, devastated,
denying the bomb that exploded
in the middle of us all.

Further back, further.
First, I must describe the father
who died.

But I cannot go further back.
I have no memory
and no words.

So I find myself
in front
of the door,
raising
my hand,
to lift the latch.

High Seas

I am sailing on high seas,
child height through damp washing.
Glimpsed through white sheets,
there's a bell in the sky that looks like a cloud,
hung to ring.

Spectral tents of billowing cool
welcome me in a rush of cracking sails.
Hooped over circles of taut lines
my vessel bucks and wheels to every breeze,
crow's nest creaking.

I sway over oceans
until the heat of the day,
steaming through ghostly cotton,
starches my game completely.

Pick Your Own

Today I am a bride
up and down the aisles of fruit,
nodding, side to side
under the veil of my tatty fringe,
best dress on despite:
'Fruit is impossible to get out'.

I find the nest of strawberries
in scratching sun-warmed straw
and silently kneel,
a devotee,
head below the hedge
to hide from my sister.

Small, hard, white, hairy
tight-seeded fruits
sit in thick leaves, waiting.
I pass those and rummage,
squashing into ashy puffs of mould,
which sigh out.

Another dive under green leaves
where large scarlet hearts,
seed-cushioned,
coyly peep, gleaming, ripe.
Bubbles of juice pop between my teeth.

Sunshine on my tongue, seeds
on my teeth, I feel the heat
on my parting, sun pouring
on my head, filling up
the cup of my brain
and spilling out through my dazed eyes,
my reddened lips.

contd…

contd…

A tiny hand through the hedge
from the other side, a giggle,
then a fight, a race, to cram
bulging and bursting fruit
into our mouths.
I win.

The weigh-in, the accounting,
Mum's studied indifference
to our lips, chins, fingers
stained and sticky.

On the homeward journey,
dog whining in car's heat.
We are pale and quiet
on slippy back seat,
finally sick
of sun and fruit.

Ten Pence For The Sea

Dragged, moaning, from my morning bed,
I pull on clothes laid out last night; neat
and ironed for our holiday, Mum said.

She lifts me onto the large leather seat
in the back. The dog steals my place
and my brother teases half-heartedly.

Headlights from cars going the other way
sweep through the dark. Her cigarette glows red
showing the frown of worry on her face.
Shivering, in a grey grit dawn-soaked dead-end,
I bite cold sausage hungrily,
first stop of the day, the dog an instant friend.

Then, ten pence for the first to see the sea!
We smell it first, wide and free, and there.
I saw it, my brother cries, but it was me

I saw it, green and blue, shifting over the bare
rock, and white spray lifting into air,
the summer air.

The First Time

A friend's pool, unchlorined,
green at the edges and in the depths,
more pond than pool,
leaves collecting, and newts flicking
in the shallow end.

My mother walks backwards,
keeping bleached hair up,
words spilling from red lips,
cigarette sticking,
as she mouths clever asides.
Laughter rises and falls around the edges.

I puff and blow and frown,
face red, hair wet and slick.
I want to cry but more,
I want to swim.

What is it that happens now?

I no longer feel the slipping hands,
elastic tight at the top of my thighs,
or slithery fronds of weeds.
Coming up like knowledge,
the water holds me.

My mother, indifferent,
or sensing the change in me,
begins to let go.
I no longer need her.
I frog kick, flutter hands and feet—
laughter again amidst cries of 'bravo'—
and, with my mother forgotten at the edge,
do a width on my own.

Orange Plastic Purse

That purse. I see it now,
orange, plastic, gold clasp,
puffed like a jelly fish,
mouth open to swallow money.

I save pennies,
which become pound notes.
Two, and one fifty pence.
Two pounds fifty, so proud.

I can buy sweets, comics,
presents for friends, and still
have change for a coke.
But I lose it.

I look in every nook and niche,
every dust-filled corner,
crumb-filled cranny,
turn up nothing.

My loss remains private.
I cannot confess my carelessness
to my mother.
Words rise but are swallowed.

Weeks later, after constant, fruitless,
searching, I pray
on my scabbed knees,
by my bed

and spot, between the mattress
and wire coils, a flash of orange.
There it is, plastic,
gold-clasped, money-filled.

contd…

contd…

I still don't believe in God,
but do believe in getting down
on your knees
every now and then.

First published online by Silver Birch Press (US) (2018)

Creature

I wasn't a girl when I was a child.
I was a creature.

I would stuff dolls into prams
and push them round the garden,
shaking them to sleep.

I would skip to the shops,
converse with fairies in the trees,
control the wind.

I would make tents from blankets,
feed worms to teddies,
look at the sun, half-eyed.

I would skip like a boxer,
knit like a fisherman,
wait for Father Christmas until my ears rang with listening
and knew it was sleigh bells.

I would walk in the night,
forget about it in the day,
inhabit a half world of sleeping.

I danced like a Spanish lady
with a real mantilla,
comb and castanets, all my size.

My cat followed me everywhere
but the dog howled at my recorder practice
and bit my sister's best friend.

contd…

contd…

I was the world's worst Brownie
who could never remember her daily good deed,
although I knew I was good every day.

I waited every night, and prayed
for my father to come home
and save me.

Every night he did
and every morning I woke up
and he was dead again.

I talked and talked at school
but, being clever,
talked my way out of it.

My hair was scraped into plaits,
pulled into ponytails
or flapped lank in the fast wind.

I outstripped my sister
on the concrete-covered playground
where tunnels scraped my knees,
banged my forehead,
hid slime and mud
and worse.

Oxo Cube (Only Beef)

Unwrap the top
of a tin foil cube,
sharp-edged.
Expose one plane
of gritty, flat brown.
Lick.

Lick and lick
until a saucer dip appears,
until the tongue is stained,
until there is a playground
of dark tongues.

Then next week
move on
to Jif lemons,
plastic, hard,
filled with water.
Spray First Years.

Laugh, long and loudly,
at anyone caught
with an Oxo cube.

Extinction

Boys were dangerous
and pathetic,
cigarettes a possibility.

Children fell off bikes
and drowned in quarries,
disappeared onto moors
and newspapers became
frightening
and fascinating.

Nothing was said and everything
understood.
War was a recent memory

and fear of extinction as hot as summer.

La Cucaraca

We practised for weeks,
every break and every lunchtime,
up, high, in the top-storey
music room.

We were in with a chance,
lost in the singing,
maracas, the triangle,
everything going for us.
We didn't hear the end-of-break bell.

Until, hours later, we spotted,
through the window,
the whole school, picking across the lawn.
Our hearts sank deeper, colder
and faster than the Titanic.

Later, teachers told us that the police
and parents were nearly called.
As it was, they had the whole school
looking for us. Hysteria rose.

—So, you think it's funny, do you?—
I couldn't speak, overcome
by the awfulness of everything.
Chantal, by my side, kept
a similar silence.

From somewhere my tiny voice said,
—But can we still play in the music competition?—
Their bark of laughter was my reply.

A grade 8 cellist won the competition
And Chantal and I never sat together again.

Fog

It's a dream,
this fog.
It wraps the car.
Winking brake lights
leak red.
Everything danger.

Traffic in the rear view
approaches,
passes,
leaves.
Our possibilities of help.

We clutch our satchels,
eat old, hidden sweets,
watch as the dark arrives.
We are cold.

Sit tight, Mum says,
it'll lift,
we'll be rescued.
Her voice wobbles.

A shadow looms,
terrorises,
then shrinks
to a policeman
in his tall hat.
Mum starts flirting.
All is well.

Horse With No Name

A song suggests itself
to my adult mind.
My eyes sting
and a half smile hovers
at the rush of thoughts,

too real to be thoughts.
Felt in the body,
the young, effortlessly skinny body
tanned, freckled,
clad in 1976 flares,
hair in mismatched bunches
not a scrap of make-up
(none to my name, then),
walking the fat Labrador
along the Winnaway,
silence, birds, silence,
just me and the sun
and a Horse With No Name
running through my mind.

Kawasaki

He guns his engine close to me.
I jump and he laughs,
rattling off a fusillade
of half-compliments,
attacking me with wisecracks.

Disorientated,
I lean on a country gate,
feel the cold moss thickening
in the splintered gaps.
He startles me and is pleased.

This is his wooing,
a persistent campaign
to catch me off guard.
Finally flattery overcomes fear
—pillion sounds glamorous—
and he takes me on his bike.
I am allowed to cut out the iconic K,
create a template, sew it on his shirt,
symbol of the road.

But, breathless in the warm sunshine,
I become tired of being scared.
I don't trust his bravado;
I am bored of being his rockchick,
sidekick, bikecandy.

He guns his engine close to me
And I wave him off one last time.

Sun

'Un petit crabbe, maman,'
a French toddler flutes,
bringing the world
to his mother.

I scan the beach with radar eyes
hidden coolly under shades,
and clock the boys on the horizon,
calculate the co-ordinates
of their throbbing presence.

My bikini straps cut in,
my legs slick with oil,
sand-glittered.

I burn, of course.
Red nose, shoulders, thighs.
Graceless with Calamine,
I watch elegant French girls
slip by to join the Young Gods
at the other end of the beach.

Weeding

Between my hand and my ear
the phone sits.

In a garden, a scraping sound
as a hoe drags over dandelion ground;
my mother, weeding.

I look around for escape
but this ghost can't see me.
Squatting over tatty beds, she sifts
the bad flowers from the good.

Fork claws scratch the stubborn surface
of the soil; hidden roots defy her work
to sprout again when her back is turned.
Her own tired measures defeat her.

Her mother, too, gardened:
loved the sunny day,
the lemonade, the secateurs
and all the roses in the wicker trug.

But it was my grandfather,
between the crafty fags in the shed,
who turned up his collar to the January wind
and fitted the spade into the cold earth, snug,
and turned the solid dark, uninteresting mud
to eventual glory.

My mother gamely tugs another ugly plant,
resisting, from its moist secrecy,
lays out this orgy of waste
to wither under the sun.

contd…

contd…

Her task seems endless, knees cracking,
hands dried in dust.
Pity, fresh and cool, wells in me.

She has to brave the winter alone;
heave the solitary spade;
because her love has been buried underground,
too deep for release, too deep to bloom again.

Between my hand and my ear
the phone sits.

Final Fitting

One mirror in the triptych
throws a picture of you,
impatient to edge me aside.
But I won't move.
I am dressing up

in your clothes, still too big
but I select velvet and silk,
slips of satin, crush of lace,
hang my new self with ropes
of sticky seed pearls.

Your mix of sham and fabulous;
spindly ankles above knifepoint heels,
tailored skirt in lurid lime.
A frivolous wig tangles my clean hair
into its cobweb nest.

Then I am finger painting;
cupid lips red and glossy
cheeks hollowed in sophistication,
lost in clouds of ancient powder.
Each face looks like yours.

I set down the brushes and sponges.
Dew-spotted, filmed with dust,
the mirror is empty now.

In this attic, junk stores the cold shadows
that creep from all the rooms below.
Your butterfly dresses, washed and ironed,
are packed into the family trunk.

Lost mornings, forgotten afternoons,
lie creased between their folds.

Fifty Years Since Sarawak

The flags of battles long ago
flutter gently in the warming draft,
and faded fringes ripple
as if recalling an ancient fray.
Horizontal, they fill
this silent, cold, stone chapel

I am here to mark a certain turn of years,
memorialise my father and find
a gentle solace in the moment.
A wave of thoughts but tears won't come.
The hum of heaters underpins the hush
and elsewhere voices echo, indistinct.

Blue spring sky shines through jewelled glass.
I blink and the jigsaw assembles into
a young St George, golden and protective,
behind each soldier, sailor, airman.

So where was he then, when my father's plane
fell from a different sky, a different time,
into that hot green jungle, far away?
Not between him and his violent death.
No.
These small words do not stand
between me and my grief.

To Crack The World

I'm tidy when I throw things,
always pick them up,
clear up the mess.

But you, brother, spent your youth
in howls of rage that chopped the air.
You bit your hand so hard it bled,
teeth badging the place.

Your anger crowbarred
grief, heavy enough
to crack the world.
You left a wake of hate;

bashed-in door, chair
struts turned to knives,
plates of Chinese staining the wall,
dog shivering.

You ran.
School after school after school.
Always brought back.
Girlfriend knocked up,
and joyrides ridden to despair.
You even stole our mother's car.

She had no answer to
the question,
'Where's my dad?'

Just all your broken things,
scattered,
around your broken heart.

My Dead Dad

My dead dad walks down the high street.
No one wears hats anymore, he notices,
and ladies wear work jeans and plimsolls.
Grown men wear PE kits
and everyone holds a telephone
with no cord, and no one meets his eye,
although he says 'Good Morning'
for the first ten minutes.

He sits on a bench and watches a beggar
drink from a paper cup.
He looks up and his heart lightens slightly;
pigeons nestle and crowd on ledges,
seagulls swoop, and clouds
move away from the sun.

My dead dad takes off his cap
and palms his slick hair neatly
behind his ears.
He smiles at his face in the shine
of his bright toe caps.
The knife-crease of his grey-blue trousers
reaches the requisite lace.

He stands and tidily replaces his cap,
shoulders straight, no hands in pockets,
medals glinting, amid the jostlers
and shovers, fat mothers, tired shop girls
on their phones, never looking up.
Although they all move out of his way.

Reviews

'Amanda's poetry has a refreshing honesty and explores the intricacies of human relationships.'
Jenny Hope —Writer. Poet. Workshop Leader and Facilitator.

'I like short collections. I like this collection. It affords the reader the opportunity to consider a group of poems as an entity, to study the visible, and discover the invisible, ties that bind them. These poems demand to be read together. Honest, cerebral, uncompromising, unsentimental, always compelling.'
Gary Longden—Staffordshire Poet Laureate (2014/2015)

I have liked Amanda's poetry ever since I've known her, and I wondered what this collection would reveal...I was not disappointed. This is a story—a lifetime—of missing someone. Amanda writes with clarity and honesty. She holds the reader from the very beginning, sharing sights, sounds and deepening emotions, leading us inexorably to her father whose early death left a cavern in her life. *Pick Your Own* is built on childhood memories, always looking for a presence that couldn't be shared. This is a pamphlet that will finish dog-eared from use. Amanda's father would be proud.
Mike Alma—Founder, Contributor and Compiler of 'Voices of 1919' (2016)